Printed in the USA

Cold Reading Technique: 23 Secrets That Psychics Don't Want You to Know

By Evan Addison

Contents

Introduction

Psychics are known to hear voices, have visions and predict the future. They can see the past and commune with the dead. Psychics can foresee imminent love relationships and dwindling bank accounts. They know all about you.

Supposedly, using their amazing powers psychics can identify information about people, places and things that is hidden from normal senses. They have ESP (extrasensory perception) or special spirit animals who clue them in to people's fortunes. When a psychic sees something, they are not talking about the tangible, like a sunrise or a plate of ravioli in front of them. They are talking about communicating with a life force beyond scientific understanding.

Psychics claim they have been given special powers, possibly from past lives or after a devastating accident or coma. Certainly psychics are part of the mainstream. It's almost impossible to turn on daytime television without finding some psychic or other divining an audience member's future. There are knock and shock TV psychics too, who appear at people's door claiming they can speak to the dead. From large urban centers where psychics can be found on practically every corner, to the Internet where a search will net more hits than a consumer can peruse in a day, psychics are part of the fabric of every day modern life.

For many people, going to the psychic is part of a weekly destination, after the grocery shopping and before lunch. For others, the spiritualist is the last house on the block as their lives are falling apart. Curiosity seekers and true believers everywhere want to know how to solve their problems, whether their ex will return, how to get a job, and what to wear to an important family function. Psychics can help anyone with anything because they know *everything*.

One thing is certain: Psychics *know* their subjects. By tapping into energy forces, they claim the power to read the thoughts of the living and commune with the dead. Medical Intuitives see virtual MRIs, and psychic detectives are often in touch with the spirits of murder victims. Physics save lives and hearts. They predict wealth and health. They solve problems and heal the downtrodden. They know the past, the present and the future.

Or do they?

Can psychics really divine the future or speak to the dead? Are they truly clairvoyant or are they just using an old magician's trick call "cold reading?" This guide will reveal the truth about psychics and the tricks of the trade they don't want you to know about when they deliver messages from the spirit world right to your front door.

Chapter 1
Cold Reading Styles

Psychics don't simply wake up one day with extraordinary powers of divination. Like any professional, psychics develop a handful of skills that work for their particular brand of cold reading. Good psychics keep their clients coming back with an appealing style and the ability to garner trust. This is no different from a chef inspiring a following with his gourmet recipes. Or a dog groomer trying to build her practice by returning happy dogs to busy owners.

Even psychics know the old adage: "If you treat a customer well, he will tell two people. If you treat a customer poorly, he will tell ten people."

Psychics, like anyone else selling a service, have their own bag of tricks to entice new clients and to keep them coming back for more. Generally speaking, most folks who seek out a psychic need help in one way or the other. And every informed psychic knows that they have to create a style of cold reading that appeals to that in a very specific way.

In the world of psychic choices, prospective customers will happen upon three common types of cold reading styles to choose from.

The Compassionate Healer, also known as the Intuitive Empath.

This is someone who knows how to use compassion and empathy to calm the client while also expressing warmth and understanding. The compassionate psychic will create a warm, cozy environment. Clients may be invited into a carefully constructed "stage" where the bookcases filled with astral leaning self-help books, many of which contain the word "love," are overshadowed by the big, comfy chairs and the small table between them draped with a lace tablecloth. Sort of like Grandma's house.

The Compassionate Healer will likely have scented candles placed strategically around the room, many of which will have the telltale drip of wax from having been burned many times before for other valuable and trusting clients. The room will feel "spiritual" with its soft lighting, warm rug and, often, a stick of incense burning near the window. The framed dragonfly and angel pictures on the wall add a blush of serenity to the room, while the choice of music is often of a new age bent; the calming sound of streams and birds against a backdrop of Celtic or eastern instrumentals like flutes or sitars. There may be a bowl of beautifully wrapped chocolates on the table and herbal tea may be in the offing.

The compassionate healer wants to make the clients feel comfortable, as if the pillowey safety of the chair is the very best place to rest her vulnerability. It is essential to the Empathic Intuitive that customers can leave their distrust at the door and enter a kingdom of kindness.

The compassionate healer will have perfected the art of projecting a sympathetic personality. They want their clients to be open and receptive; they want to convey the idea that a reading is a team effort. The Compassionate Healer is both mentor and mom, the customer is both student and child.

This type of cold reading requires that the psychic use a soft, comforting voice. Her body language is non-confrontational: gentle eye contact, an agreeable smile and an alert listening pose. Perhaps her head is cocked sympathetically to one side while the sitter speaks. Her arms and legs remain uncrossed. There's no armoring here.

Psychics will almost always start with what is known as a "character reading." The Empathic Intuitive will often use flattery to comfort the visitor and gather information. So it is important that a cold reading begin with a statement that is generous and helpful. An example might be: "You have so much love inside of you but the people around you don't seem to appreciate that about you."

Immediately the sitter is reassured. It's nice to be right and it's especially validating to know that everyone else is wrong.

All of this is not to say that every psychic has honed her compassion skills set strictly to manipulate her visitor into a return visit. After all, psychics are people too, and many people have empathy and compassion for others. The Intuitive Empath, however, is absolutely aware of how she uses her compassion quotient and has likely perfected her skills at flattery and kindness to endear customers to her, and to bring them back "home" for more.

The No Sugarcoating Guide

The operative word in this style of cold reading is "guide." A guide knows everything. For instance, you want your back-country nature guide to know CPR, to be educated about dangerous wildlife and poisonous plants and, if necessary, to be handy with a leg split, should your tibia snap while you try to outdistance a bear.

The straight shooting cold reader is this kind of guide; someone who can cold read you out of a bad financial choice and, as a skilled marksman, has dead aim on your career choices. He is a master at tough love. He will handle the sitter in a stern and serious manner with the intent to help her in the long run. This no-holds barred approach takes some skill because the cold reader of this particular style must be careful not to scare the client away. The ultimate theme for this psychic is that he has to go a little hard on you, but he will save you a heap of heartache in the end.

The client who chooses this type of psychic is already predisposed to the notion that the tough love approach is the only *objective* way to glean an accurate reading. In fact they have to believe that objectivity is actually a true component of a cold reading, otherwise they'd more likely step into the office of a medical doctor for healing.

Clients who visit the No Sugarcoating Guide are people who are used to tough love. Maybe they grew up in a military family. Usually they are people parenting difficult children, married to alcoholic husbands or suffocating in crushing relationships. Their co-dependence is killing them. And they've come to the right place because their spiritualist is the Joe Friday of cold readings. "Just the facts, ma'am."

To that end, this type of cold reader wants to appear credible and yet distantly caring. However, his objective is not to hold a sob-fest or a therapy session, but rather to tell people what they want to know as objectively and completely as possible. This psychic uses his logical approach as a selling point and will go all out to show the client that he is practical and accurate.

The sitter in this case may walk into an "office style" room, replete with leather chairs, bank lighting and framed psychic school diplomas hanging on the clean white walls. The bookshelves will be filled with titles like "Thinking Your Way Past Your Past" or "A Psychic's Science for Ending Co-Dependence." There might be a dictionary on a stand, and a magnifying glass.

There will not be chocolate on the table. Healthy choices are the only choices for this cold reader. You might find gluten free cookies or a jar of nuts on the table, which will likely appear to be untouched. That's because this isn't a social visit.

The cold read begins with few preambles. This psychic is all business. His handshake is strong, meant to convey the notion that there will be no warm hugs at this cold reading. He is business-like or sternly paternal. He might tell the client how brave she is to come, adding that no one in the profession can give as accurate and truthful a reading as he will. He may establish that the client is there to deal with a messy or perplexing situation and will address it in a way that shows he won't tiptoe around the problem. He might say something like this: "I know how difficult and painful the truth is, but in the end it's better to face reality than to wrestle with fantasy."

As a guide who doesn't mince words, this psychic will want you to know how intelligent his insight is. He may wear glasses, and sit across from you with attentiveness and strong eye contact. Or he may bend over, elbows on his knees, face in his hands as he concentrates on your energy field. He is the coach who knows the game, knows you are losing it and who won't sugar coat your problem or the tough choices you will need to make to win the game. Practical action is what this type of psychic will offer, conveying to the client that magical thinking will get them nowhere.

The sitter will note this psychic's intelligence and seriousness. She will feel safe. It may hurt, but she is in good hands.

The Middle Ground Psychic

Truth is, most psychics will convey a mix of tough love and compassion. In other words, the sitter might be greeted with incense burning *and* a dictionary on a stand. There will be pleasant landscape prints on the wall, plus a certificate from the Arthur Findlay College of Pyschic Science.

It's safe to say that being a psychic centrist is probably the most effective way to garner clients and keep them coming back for more. This psychic has an elegant plan: to postulate solutions based on common sense while using gentle truisms about human nature in a way that allows the client to apply them personally and find meaning in them.

The moderate psychic, if you will, is both empathetic and on the level. They use their clairvoyance to convince the client that they can tap into their own command center of clarity, intuition and empowerment. In other words the science behind the psychic is steeped in the strategies of a balanced cold read but there's love and compassion in every word. The tools associated with compassion are meshed with the straight shooting skills of the ER physician performing triage.

Middle Ground psychics prefer to convey an ideology of practical and reasonable solutions handed out with empathy and kindness. They practice an apologetics of a sort, defending their techniques by presenting a rational basis for them in the unselfish interests of meeting the client's needs. They are both guide and partner to the sitter's search for financial freedom, health solutions or relationship woes. They will appear to identify with the client using the skills of compassion and empathy, while at the same time offer hard-hitting advice and the sometimes cold reality of "the truth."

The middle ground psychic tangoes her way through the s field, she is adept at making quick assumptions, followed by even speedier corrections should she err. Humor is the most effective tool in her kit. She can comfort you while you cry, then give it to you straight. The client will emerge with a sense that their unseeing eyes have been opened by a kindly aunt who, nevertheless, earned her street smarts in the school of hard knocks.

Chapter 2
Stages of the Cold Reading

Most psychics work through the three stages of cold readings like professional dancers. The dancer's job is to appear effortless as she floats across the stage. Her technical proficiencies may appeal to the connoisseur of dance, but usually for the lay person, the appeal is aesthetic. Their emotions are the main target.

One of the most important skills that effective money-making psychics acquire is the ability to appear totally in control and knowledgeable at all times, but never "practiced" as if they've simply rehearsed their technique for the benefit of their wallets. How they gain the trust of their clients and a repeat visit involves knowing how to traverse the three stages of the cold read.

A - Getting Acquainted

Meeting a client for the first time seems like the easiest task in the world; just be nice and offer them a beverage. But the first stage of the cold reading requires a lot more than mere pleasantries. It is perhaps the most important part of the cold read. It requires the finesse of a high wire artist and the cunning of a coyote. The psychic is investing time and energy strictly for the client, and the client is the star of the show. Those psychics who give successful cold readings have honed their art down to a science

One thing the psychic knows is that the client is there because he is a believer. But the psychic has to reel the client's faith in and keep it alive. The first thing that a cold reader must do is create a warm and comfortable rapport with the client. The psychic has entered the no man's land of gaining trust. To that end, she must convince the client that the two of them are in this journey together; that the psychic can't do all the work. One of the first things she might say to her new client is "Throughout the reading there may be a lot of things that make sense to you more so than to me. Please try to connect to what I'm saying while I channel and you will see the relevance to your life."

In other words, we're in this together, but I'm the pro.

The talented psychic will explain the most important aspects of her trade. She will tell clients, in a warm and convincing voice that she "reads" the energy of the client. That energy is akin to something like the client's soul. And the true energy of the soul is to be respected. The psychic respects the client.

At this acquaintance stage, the psychic will also need to pre-rationalize the misses she will invariably make in her cold reading. So she might come out and say, perhaps with a sigh signaling her many arduous years of practice, "I would love to say that I can predict the future 100%. But no one is perfect. Even Joe Namath fumbled the ball sometimes." This puts the client at ease. Even a psychic is human. But what the client may not suspect is that by saying this, the psychic is preparing the client for the misreads she is bound to make.

Finally, before moving onto the next stage, the psychic will show her appreciation for how difficult it must be to require her services. She will make sure her first-time clients know they are not alone. Everyone of her multitude of customers, she will testify, have come to her with heavy hearts. It's human nature to go through happy times *and* difficult times. And it is her job and her *calling* to be a helping person. Her intuition will make the customer feel better, will give him a course of action, and alleviate the client's worry, just as she has for the countless others who have come to her beforehand.

It's always important for the psychic to play dumb in the smartest way possible. Before she moves on, she might say, "throughout this reading, the results will make sense more to you than they do to me."

This tactic of appearing unassuming, modest even, is a subtle way of conveying to the sitter that she doesn't even have to know you to really *know* you. She's that good. But more importantly, she is setting the sitter up to personalize and make meaning out of her insight even though it is so general that pretty much everyone on the planet upon hearing it would think it's specific to them.

B. Examining the Issue

Every experienced psychic knows that there are seven themes most people want to talk about: Love, health, money, career, travel, education and ambitions. Sometimes two or more are fused together such as health and travel, or education and professional ambition. But generally speaking these topics are front and center of every reading.

At this stage of meeting the customer, the cold reader employs a technique known as fishing. The client is vitally important in this phases of the reading. He is the psychic's Rock of Gibraltar because she will imperceptibly extract information from him and use it to build the foundation for her cold read. Without these building blocks for a strong foundation, the client will be powerless to later gain a customer's confidence and perform a "successful" reading. Every psychic knows the failed cold read lies in the black hole of misinformation or worse, no information at all.

The trick here is for the psychic not to appear as if he is interrogating the client or gathering information. The point of all cold readings is the fabulous mystery of the psychic's intuition. He has to appear as if he just *knows* the client without seeming to ply her with questions. This is the skill of the detective in the interrogation room who knows that it's all more or less a confidence game involving manipulation and subtle cues during which the suspect will continue to make incriminating statements without even realizing it.

In the psychic's studio, the cold reader relies on a simple psychological idea; that human beings all have the ability to make sense of data, no matter what it is and no matter how limited it might be. The psychic is akin to the car dealer who latches on to the idea that the buyer doesn't just want that spiffy red Mercedes but actually cannot live without it.

Similarly the psychic banks on the client's willingness to a) find more meaning in a situation than there actually is and b) connect the dots to make sense for *themselves* what the cold reader brings up, in spite of the fact that all psychics know that anyone can make anything personal to themselves if they are so inclined. The fact that the sitter is, well, sitting there, implies they are favorably disposed to believe intuition over hard science. The psychic knows this.

There is an actual name for this self-validating tendency of the clients. It's called the Barnum effect, named after the American showman who founded Barnum and Baileys circus. Though in truth Barnum did not coin the saying, he is often attributed as having said, "There's a sucker born every minute."

This is not to say that people who go to a psychic are "suckers" or stooges. People are always looking for meaning in their lives, especially when the chips are down. And it is often a sign of emotional survival and creativity to find meaning in statements that might be posed by a psychic.

A study conducted in March of 1975, and published in *Psychology Today* demonstrated that a random group of people (in this case college students) who were given the same exact astrological forecast all were impressed at how accurate it was for them individually. Moreover, when a select few of them were asked to explain in more detail why they thought the horoscope was accurate, they were found to believe the horoscope sounded even more accurate and pertinent after discussing why.

So if you think a psychic versed in the art of cold reading isn't aware of the accurate notion that human beings will ascribe personal meaning to a broad analysis or prediction, think again. Not only does a skilled psychic know this, she knows exactly how to sway the direction of the reading so the client is left convinced that the diagnosis is meant only for him. It's a life changer. The client is usually incredulous. How could the psychic know him that well? She certainly has a mysterious gift.

The way to fish for information will be discussed in more detail later, but for now it's safe to conclude that general questions, often disguised as statements, will give the psychic enough information to go on with the reading. For the psychic it's a cakewalk.

C. Making a Prediction/Diagnosis

After all the prep work, the slicing and dicing, the managing and the molding, the psychic must bring it home. The bases are loaded and she's up at bat. It's now time to swing into the prediction or the intuitive "diagnosis" aspect of the cold read. Surgery is over. The patient is waiting for the news. This may even be one area in which the psychic trumps the physician where bedside manner is concerned.

She is always hopeful and positive to the client. Why else would anyone go to a psychic but for hope? A good therapist would make you work too hard and a medical doctor might have performed a successful operation but will also make sure you know the multiplicity of deleterious side effects, possible bad outcomes and days of torment ahead for the patient following that tonsillectomy.

Here the trick is to turn a bad situation into a positive one. It's the psychic's way of bowing down to the goddess of old adages: "Every dark cloud has a silver lining." So she might say something like "your bankruptcy will be a stressor on your finances for a while, but a new, exciting job is just around the corner."

Notice that she doesn't say, "You will find a bag of money that will go unclaimed." The psychic knows all about keeping it real. To any rational person the awesome stroke of good luck she is predicting will raise the banner of skepticism. People understand that no one, not even a psychic, can promise such speedy results. Something like this prediction would have the opposite effect of lightening the load on the client's shoulders. It would probably get them started on the road to refund. Whether or not it seems true, people want to work a little for positive outcomes. They may believe in the probability for a good future after having to work at it for awhile, but they won't believe in magical thinking.

You might check out the websites of psychics and find yourself surprised at how superlative their reviews are. Four and half, five stars everywhere. On all the sites you've checked out. There are many reasons for this, not the least of which is that the psychic more often than not has her website set up so that she can pick the reviews she wants to post. But more importantly, these exalted recommendations are more likely real because the proficient psychic has answered her clients' prayers. And believing that your prayers have been answered is certainly a good feeling to have. It's not about whether the prediction comes true – most customers post their praise immediately after the psychic reader has inspired warm feelings within them and long before the predictions do or don't come true. What clients are responding to is the hope the psychic had given them, not the truth of the outcomes.

Finally, what most people want is to be comforted, to know that their love lives will heal, their finances will sort out, their children will be safe on their trip to Africa. They want to be told everything will be all right. We are all looking for that assurance because, face it, life is a bumpy road and sometimes the tires are flat.

Some people approach a psychic because their present situations have become intolerable. They think their boss is reading their emails, or their best friend is having an affair with their wife. Maybe they worry about having enough money to pay for surgery or fear that the IRS will audit them.

Usually what the psychic sees in t every day problems versus potential future problems is yet more opportunity. They will give their client a reality check answer. "Yes, I see that it is possible the IRS will audit you." But that yes is the gateway to positive outcomes and a happy client. "At the same time, you will use you experience to understand your tax liability, and make a small fortune in a new business enterprise."

In the end, the expert cold reader takes her training seriously. She knows when to capitalize on information gleaned or given up spontaneously, she is your guide, your mentor, your best friend. She can raise your spirits even if the news isn't perfect or the rewards won't be immediate. And most of all, she gives you props. Without your own intuitive powers, she never would have been able to help you.

Chapter 3
Why Cold Reading Works

Why do people go to psychics?

Some would say because that's what you do in Vegas on vacation.

Perhaps the better question is: Why does cold reading work?

The short answer is that people want to feel better.

Imagine your spouse has just died and now the taxman is knocking on your door. You've been to a therapist, but it was costly and ineffective. You have a good job, you've got a college degree and a nice house. No one would call you shallow or flighty. Desperate, maybe. But not a pushover. At the same time, you might be open- minded to healing. There are alternatives to Xanax. The self-help gamut runs from psychiatrists, to silent retreats in the desert, to the Botanica downtown where you can pick up some Mexican healing herbs and a statue of the Virgin Mary.

To many people in distress or pain, a psychic somehow falls in the middle of extremes and expenses. These people have likely seen psychics on TV and have marveled about their astounding powers, their kindness and their plain-spoken no-nonsense approach to fixing problems. The cherry on the cake is that they seem so intuitive. How could they possibly know someone they've never met? Yet they do!

So perhaps the real answer to why cold readings work is that clients *believe* they work. Coupled with the need for solutions to their problems, the psychic, to many people, is someone who has super powers of divination, the solutions to problems and the bedside manner of a saint.

Also, think about it. In the realm of other-worldly phenomenon, psychics have had a long history, dating back to ancient times. Astrologers go back to the 4th century BC. Seers and prophets are sprinkled throughout The Bible. The Delphic Oracle, one of the earliest stories in classical antiquity dating back to the 8th century BC, is nothing short of a tale of prophetic abilities.   And Nostradamus, a French apothecary and seer who is known worldwide even today for his book, *Les Prophities* published in 1555, is credited with predicting major world events.

The 1960s with its palm readers and crystal balls, gave way to the New Age spirituality of the 70s, and the subsequent present-day commercial refinement of psychics and fortune-tellers. The cold read has formed out of the past where it eventually dug its hooks into 21st century modern culture. It now enjoys a healthy life. Psychics are all around us, as characters in Marvel Comic books to Stephen King novels. The television psychics and the psychic on the corner flashing her phone number in green neon over her door, is now a part of our common visual field. Psychics pay a part in our shared history and today have been normalized as part of our daily lives. In a world that often feels like it's crushing us, depleting our spirits and scaring us, a psychic doesn't seem so weird.

The cold reading, which is not one simple trick but a host of practical tools in a big psychic kit, works because it's a seemingly effortless method that produces huge benefits in a short amount of time with a reasonable amount of money. People see that the outcomes far outweigh the cost and energy of seeing a psychic. The lucky few get a free cold read on television talk shows. But for the average person, the Internet or the corner market cold read is the answer to their woes. It's more "scientific" than prayer, and less expensive than a psychiatrist. The skilled psychic has perfected the art of the cold read and clients know that she will pick them up from the heap they've fallen into. They will commune with loved ones from the beyond, they will predict jobs and love, and they will do well because based on their psychic abilities they know you. Everyone can see that. You are not taking a number at the deli here. You're someone special.

Chapter 4
Cold Reading Techniques

The previous discussion on cold reading techniques requires a little more exploration, not just because it's fascinating in and of itself, but because it reveals just how "intuitive" a psychic is. Intuitive about what techniques to hone into a science, that is.

One note: there is much scientific evidence and discussion about a human's ability to intuit situations and outcomes. Intuition is a wonderful and very well-researched aspect of the human experience.

Studies have found that when it comes to making major life decisions, such as which house to buy or which person to marry, trusting your intuition leads to better outcomes than trusting your logical, thinking brain.

One study found that car buyers who had plenty of time to pour over all of the information about their various car choices were later found to be satisfied with their purchase only 25% of the time. Meanwhile, 60% of buyers who made a quick, intuitive decision about their car purchase were found to be satisfied with their purchase.

So it would be wrong to scoff at the idea of intuition. When you need to make a life decision and you have two choices, you will feel your heart pounding and your palms sweating when you lean into the wrong choice. This is your clue to act intuitively by literally listening to your heart.

It must be remembered if you visit a psychic that though she may very well have as much intuition as you do, she is also trained in using techniques that will make you think she is intuitively smarter than you and knows everything about you. Techniques are not the same thing as intuition. As will be discussed below, the psychic's "skill" at divination is directly proportional to how well she knows the techniques, many of which are based on known psychological factors that have been studied and widely reported by scientists throughout the years.

Psychics always use common sense. If you want someone to trust you, you are kind, gentle, and most of all, a kindred spirit. This is often conveyed by a welcoming smile, and if necessary, an empathic pat on the shoulder.

Stage A – Getting Acquainted Techniques

The empathic intuitive's very first step is to establish a connection with the client that is warm, flattering and trusting.

Interestingly, a psychic's marketing strategy factors into this first stage. If a psychic has branded himself as one who doesn't sugar coat his cold read, then he will likely skip this stage and move on. His way of commitment to the sitter is to be authoritative and commanding. He will welcome the client in with a businesslike handshake, ask what the issue is and dive right in.

But for the compassionate healer, getting acquainted is the foundation upon which the cold read is built.

For this psychic, a warm greeting is compulsory. She will be gentle and sympathetic from the start. Then she will guess the reason for the sitter's visit. She already knows that most people visit a psychic for relationship or career issues, and quite often because they want to commune with a loved one who has passed. She will rely on statistics and make a guess about the reasons for the visit. But instead of choosing one reason (this would never work because the odds of getting it right are stacked against her) she will say, "I sense you're here to talk about relationships or your job. But I'm also sensing some grief."

Notice how she won't say, "I'm sensing that you've lost a loved one." She would never nail it that closely because that would be statistical suicide. Specificity is the psychic's chicken pox. She will stay away from it at all costs.

But she knows that "grief" is a general emotion. It isn't always about the loss of a loved one. Grief enters into many situations: A shaky or dissolving relationship, a lost job, a missing pet. So she isn't wrong. In fact, throwing the G-word into the mix makes her more right – she knows that most folks are coming to her because life's bowl of cherries have currently spoiled.

The client will be amazed. Yes! This is exactly what he's come for. And if it's just the job issue, then that's what he will have heard the psychic say. The psychic knows that people will hear what they need to hear and discard the rest. They will believe what they need to believe. They will construe the words to fit their life. And most importantly this reasoning and acceptance will take one millisecond for the client's brain to arrive at it.

Having now established her astonishing gift, the intuitive psychic will use the very same strategy to deepen the session. The "general statement" strategy, for lack of a better word, will almost always work. Again, what the psychic knows is that the client will personalize an otherwise wide-ranging, practically universal statement. In other words this customer will ignore the obvious generality of the statement and be amazed at how precisely it applies to him alone.

So, for example. You've walked into the lovingly appointed studio of the kindly psychic (almost like your Aunt Ruthie's living room, God rest her soul) and she's already divined your problem. Your marriage has gone sour.

Now the psychic leans over. She travels to Supernatural City. She opens her eyes, and conveying astonishment, she says, "I see an important woman in your life."

Everyone has a woman that is important in their lives. Perhaps for this client, the woman is the person her husband jilted her for. The client will look at the psychic with excitement. She will acknowledge this woman's existence and exclaim her wonder. How could a perfect stranger possibly know about Janice, the adulterer who stole her husband and left her bereft?

The psychic is probably the only one in the room who knows the answer to that question.

Stage B – Gone Fishing

Fishing for information is one of those necessary skills that psychics must learn and perfect in order to make any money at their job. It constitutes about two thirds of the cold read and is meant to further instill a sense of trust while it keeps the reading alive. Without information the psychic can't perform a cold read. Information is the gravy on the potatoes.

The main goal of the fishing expedition is to steer the boat to the right watering hole, hopefully where all the little fish are swimming around just waiting to be the main dish at the dinner table.

1.   The Barnum (or Forer) Effect

Every psychic who has ever gone to psychic school and every psychic who hasn't, knows the beauty and efficacy of the so-called Barnum Effect, sometimes also known as the Forer effect.

As previously described, it is a technique at convincing people that something is true or real when it's not. It is often credited to P.T.

Barnum, of Barnum and Bailey circus fame who is considered by many as a master manipulator. Barnum was said to have claimed "We have something for everybody."

Others refer to it as the Forer Effect so named after the psychologist Bertram Forer who died in 2000.

Forer found that people tend to accept vague and general statements as uniquely fit to them.

In 1948, Forer gave a personality test to his students, ignored their answers and presented everyone with the above evaluation. When asked to rate the accuracy on a scale of 1-5, with 5 being most accurate, the class average was 4.2. This test has been repeated hundreds of times since 1948 and the evaluations are still the same; 4.2 out of 5 or 84% accurate.

His exactness wowed his students. Then he told them he used a newsstand astrology column as the basis of his evaluation. What he did, in the end, was convince his student subjects that he could read their character.

This is what the psychic is doing the entire time of the cold read. She is basically convincing her client that, with the help of spirit guides and energy sources, she can read your character. What she knows, and what Forer knew, as do all showmen and women like P.T. Barnum, is that people are vain and optimistic. They often are possessed of wishful thinking and some amount of gullibility. What they are concerned with, by the time they are visiting a psychic, is the *desire* for claims of truth rather than empirical evidence that what a psychic *says* is the truth. Statements that are positive or flattering are very easy to accept. Psychics trade in emotions; they bank on uncertainty and hope.

What the sitter wants is to make sense of all the disconnected information that he faces daily; information that is all the more baffling while in the midst of crisis. The psychic has the perfect answer and the exact set of skills to "help" her client. All psychics, no matter their styles, empathic or all business, have one skill in common: They will bombard the client with so many disconnected question so rapidly that they give the impression they have access to personal information about their subjects.

This is where the Barnum Effect enters the picture, or shall we say, the crystal ball.

There are standard Barnum Effect phrases such as:

You want a particular amount of change and variety

When confronted with restrictions and obstructions you feel upset and fearful.

You are a rational person, priding yourself on sufficient evidence rather than blind, random statements.

Your independent thinking has been both a boon and a challenge for you in your personal and professional life.

Above all else, you desire security.

While you do have a few character weaknesses, your positive qualities more than compensate for them.

Sometimes you question whether you made the right decision or not.

You know how to be a good friend, but at times you wish you were more popular and at ease in your interpersonal relationships.

You are frequently extroverted, approachable and sociable while at other times you are introverted, cautious and reserved.

Example 1

Psychic: Losing a parent can be tough, but I can see that you are the sort of person who comes out of tragedies a little bit stronger and a little bit wiser.

Client: It's true. I'm learning so much more about my dad since he died, and it's helping me to honor his memory rather than mourn his passing.

Psychic: This is one of the hardest things anyone can go through, but you should know your father has passed to the other side and he is so proud of you for how you've been bolstering other people up even when you yourself have been so emotional.

Client: Really? I'm trying to be there for my mother especially, because she took it so hard. There have been times where I smiled through the tears because I was the only one holding it together at the viewing and the funeral...

Example 2

Psychic: Change is difficult, but you are the type of person who can eventually find their way and reach a point where you are comfortable.

Client: Sometimes it does take me a while to get there, but yes, I learn to adapt.

Psychic: This is why you have come to me. Something has shifted or will shift and you are afraid of what it could mean.

Client: Just so. I'm thinking about switching jobs...

Psychic: You're a hard worker who makes a positive impact by giving your all on projects about which you feel passionately. You don't give up, especially when you are so near to the finish line...

Client: Oh! I'll get a big bonus if I stick around until next year at this current job.

2.   Shotgunning

In the world of firearms a shotgun, also known as a scattergun and a peppergun is fired from the shoulder and typically uses the energy of a fixed shell to fire a wad of pellets, called shot, at the target. The scattered shot, especially fired at close range can be devastating. Usually one or more of the projectiles manages to hit the target.

Shotgunning in the universe of psychics is aptly named. It allows them to throw out a slew of information, during which the psychic watches for body language and other physical reactions to narrow the scope of their cold read. Expert cold readers can "shotgun" at a blinding speed of about one bait per second.

The principle of this technique, much like the reason for using a shotgun to, say, take a bird out of the sky, is that the psychic is bound to hit on something. Shotgunning works very well for psychics who are doing cold readings to large groups, as on talk shows.

Here is an example of shotgunning, which includes a series of vague statements dispersed in rapid fire:

"There's a heart problem, I'm sensing an older male figure, father figure, grandfather or...maybe an uncle. I'm feeling chest pain and sensing a health issue involving the heart of a male in your family..."

The psychic already knows that heart disease is the leading cause of death in the world. And she doesn't say which relative it is specifically. She will also note the age of the subject and based on her reasoning will suggest father or grandfather, or both, just to cover all bases.

Example 1

Psychic: There is someone at your place of work, someone…jealous, a rival or someone who is kind of a pill to you for no reason. They're about your age or maybe even a little bit older, and they seem to look at you like you're competition for work or attention from the boss…

Client: Oh my God. There's this woman in my department who is kind of a jerk to everyone, but she especially seems to hate me for some reason!

Psychic: Yes, yes. She's catty, has a hard time making friends with people at the company, can't seem to get the praise that you do, and so she focuses her negativity at you in the hopes of dragging you down with her.

Client: I thought I was crazy, but she always does seem to go after me when she needs someone to take out her frustrations.

Example 2

Psychic: I'm seeing a strong female presence, a close friend or a sister, perhaps even an aunt or a mother-figure, and flowers…lots of flowers, and there are tears. Happy tears, sad tears, it's not entirely clear, but there is a strong bond of sisterhood or womanhood pulsing through the event…

Client: Oh my gosh! My sister is getting married this summer, and I'm planning her shower.

Psychic: Yes, that's right, it's the bond of true sisterhood that I am sensing. The tears are yours, because you are happy for your sister, but you also fear that her marriage will change your special relationship.

Client: She has moved across the country for him already…what if I lose her to him?

3.   The Small Statement

As any fisherman knows, without a net, you can't catch more than one fish. This is true for the psychic. The fact is, the psychic doesn't have a net. She has a rod and some bait. Hence the reasons she will begin gathering information using the client. In this phase, the psychic will home in on the customer's issue by referencing things that would probably apply to most people. It's careful, patient work.

After the acquaintance phase where the psychic makes an accurate guess then applies the generic statements, she will know what to fish for. She might see, for instance, that the ring finger of the client has a tan line demonstrating where her band used to rest before her husband's dalliance ended her marriage. She will know that the client's particular problem is likely that the husband is no longer in the picture and the client herself knows why. She will begin gathering intelligence while keeping a close eye on the client. The sitter's body language and expressions are clues to the psychic about whether she happens to be on the right line of questioning.

She begins with something that is both vague and suggestive. To use the detective analogy again, this tactic works by using a statement as a kind of leading question, whereby the perp jumps in with a denial that reveals the opposite of his repudiation, or he may go right into inadvertently admitting, by way of subtle trickery, some aspect of his crime.

This ambiguous and nonspecific statement might be something like "I'm sensing the month of June, here." If the client appears confused and says, "I can't think of anything particular about June," the psychic might respond by saying, "That's odd because June is coming up very strongly here," and then switch directions.

But let's say the client does respond. She says that she got married in June. Picking the month of June was not a random choice for the psychic. She did the research and learned that June is the weddingist month of the year.

So after the customer acknowledges, possibly with a tear or two, that her anniversary is in June, the psychic will say, "Yes, I can see that. It was coming through very clearly here." In short, the psychic will continue to reinforce her hit thereby convincing the sitter of her astounding powers.

At this stage the psychic will expand the client's statement and develop it to make it stronger, based off of the information gathered from the client. The psychic will use her skills to repeat back the information that the customer has given her by embellishing it and making it seem like she is sensing ever new information. In truth, what the psychic is doing is simply using the repetition of a single idea to make it seem like she knows so much more than she does.

If the client has brought a friend or relative along, then making a hit is golden for the psychic. Later, maybe as they drive home, the client and her friend will talk about how accurate she was from the beginning. They will tell two friends, and so on, and so on.

The non-specific statement isn't just some haphazard declaration. The great psychic will have done her homework and commit facts and statistics to memory that she can pull out of her crystal ball when necessary. She will likely be able, if asked, to rattle off the most common female and male names, or the most common items that are left around people's houses like newspaper clippings, unpaid bills, grocery lists and boxes of disorganized photos. There are themes to learn, digest and remember such as the aforementioned relationship-career-grief continuum. There are statistics to commit to memory: Half of all marriages fail, one in every 12 adults suffer from chemical dependency, Paris is the number one vacation spot in the world, Maui the fifth.

These statistics and others that are similar in the fishing phase are the most efficacious types of bait used to both give the psychic the information she needs to move into later stages of the cold read and establish her credibility.

Example 1

Psychic: This might sound crazy, but I'm getting a sense of…diamonds…some sort of jewelry, but really diamonds are coming through very powerfully to me. A pair of earrings or perhaps a ring?

Client: Oh my God. Well, I caught my boyfriend looking at one of my rings a few months ago, like he was trying to find out the size…is he going to propose?!

Psychic: My feeling that this diamond aura surrounds you could actually be how much you want him to propose, and how much you feel that it is the right time to settle down. You have never felt this way about anyone before, have you?

Client: No, he's…he's amazing. This will be our fifth Christmas together, and we've never been stronger.

Example 2

Psychic: This might be a shock for you, but I am getting a very clear picture of a baby. A very new baby or a baby not yet born. Are you pregnant?

Client: (laughing) I hope not. I've been single for years.

Psychic: Hmm…that's interesting, but there is definitely a baby close to you or the desire for one…

Client: Wait! My ex just had a baby. I saw it online…I guess I kind of always thought that would he would be *my* husband, and that having a baby would be *my* life by now…

Psychic: Ahh, yes. Though you know you are not 100 percent ready for that responsibility, the desire to be part of your own family unit is nonetheless in the back of your mind quite often, isn't it?

Client: (sniff) It is…

4.   Flattery

Part two of the fishing trip, sometimes referred to as examining the information, is how the psychic will effectively use flattery. She certainly doesn't want to come across as fawning. And appearing obsequies or people-pleasing in any way is the apocalypse in the world of cold reading.

So there are many factors that go into using flattery. The misuse of flattery might be excessively complimenting a client and ingratiating oneself so as to appear insincere. Obviously sincerity for the psychic is of foremost importance and anything less than that will sink a cold reading.

In the jilted wife case, the psychic may comfort the client by bringing up positive character traits that anyone would like to hear about themselves. The woman who "stole" her husband is a liar and a thief. This is unlike the client whose honesty and intelligence is obvious.

"Think about it," the psychic may say, "You are graceful, beautiful and kind, attributes that would certainly incite the other woman into action. Her jealousy of you probably drove her to act so heinously. She can't take your innate goodness away from you, but her self-esteem and duplicity would enable her to take the next best thing, your husband."

This statement coming from the psychic works expertly to expand and broaden the cold read while at the same time it indulges the sitter with sweet talk and praise. Basically the psychic is saying that this type of true honesty and kindness that the client exhibits is practically unattainable for regular people, and jealousy will drive others to hurt you. The psychic might add, "This isn't fair, but it wouldn't happen to you if you weren't also a strong and capable woman." The client will nod thoughtfully, and the positive prediction about her future will then follow.

Telling the customer she is right is a brilliant form of flattery that almost always works. Obviously everyone wants to be right. And the psychic is careful not to spout forth a random compliment, but rather is actually *contextualizing* how smart the client is.

The sitter may come up with a thought in response to the psychic. This statement from the client is usually a kind of reiteration or compliment to something the psychic has already "sensed" from the client's "energy." And by telling the sitter she is spot on and quite insightful for noticing something, invites the client into a special partnership with the psychic, one that only the two of them alone can share. There's nothing like intimacy and validation to create a psychic-sitter union that will almost always guarantee a return visit.

Example 1

Psychic: You are normally comfortable making tough decisions, aren't you? No one - but especially a woman working in a man's world - reaches the point where two employers are basically vying for her without having impressive strength of mind and will.

Client: It's true, I usually know exactly what to do, especially in my professional life. But in this...I'm lost. If I stay, there's a clear path where I rise in the company year after year. But if I go...this other job has tons of travel opportunities and the work is fresh and exciting. I'm completely torn.

Psychic: For a confident, poised woman like you, there is professional success waiting, either way. You have that unique combination of work ethic and creativity that makes coworkers not a little bit jealous. You have probably overheard them complaining about your natural gifts...conversations that stopped abruptly when you walked into the room.

Client: (smiling) It has happened...

Psychic: But it can be petty and even annoying for someone who is just doing their job; you can't help it that you do it better than them, naturally.

Client: Ugh, that is true. And you know, being around all that negative energy has really started to drag me down.

Example 2

Psychic: The room lit up with your aura the second you walked in. There is a luminous quality to you that everyone has already seen, but it is especially bright now that you are engaged.

Client: Thank you! I am SO excited.

Psychic: As you should be. I am getting some of the most beautiful imagery – flowers, a gorgeous dress, the perfect setting. But more beautiful than everything else is your radiance from within. Weddings are important, but what matters is that you have the qualities that will make a marriage last forever.

5.   Making the Client Part of the Process

Everyone likes to be included. Everyone likes to feel that somehow they have contributed to a positive outcome, that in fact without them, the important result of a problem or situation would never have been possible.

Studies show, in fact that when researchers (and who is not a better researcher than a psychic) asked people to help them, they were rated more favorably than with the control group where the researcher did not ask for help.

So what does the psychic do? Obviously she won't ask to borrow the client's car. But she will couch a favor of sorts into her reading, usually somewhere near the onset of the initial meeting. This favor, as it were, takes the form of telling the client that she, the psychic, cannot do the reading alone, without the full engagement and complements of the sitter. Does that sound counterintuitive? The way it works is one of the most surprising but clever tricks in all of cold reading.

The cold reader will begin by saying that she has a gift to sense or hear what the client's needs are. Perhaps she has spirit guides who speak to her, or she "feels" loneliness or fear in her "heart chakra." Whatever the case, she will also invite the sitter in, making it sound like a favor.

She will likely explain how this gift works. Every psychic is different. While one may have spirit guides, another can read auras. She will also make sure the client knows this cold reading is confidential. She understands how trusting the client must be in order to receive a spot on reading. So she promises never to break her anonymity or reveal her secrets.

Then, after explaining her amazing powers, she will dive in, making the client feel part of the experience. She will say, "While my powers have been honed and protected over the many years of practice, sometimes all the spirits reveal to me are a series of images or symbols that have no clear connection to me – but will make perfect sense to you."

In others words, she is like an interpreter who can translate each of the words but not understand the sentence as a whole.

She will then ask, as if you are doing her a huge favor, if you can now open your heart and your mind to the possibilities of what will be revealed.

"This is a collaborative effort," she will say. "You are more than just a passive listener. Without your willingness and help, I can't give you a complete reading."

She can then give the client a few broad or vague descriptions, descriptions that could mean anything to anyone, but she will infer that, although the exact message is obscured to the cold reader, together they should mean something to the client. The client is, at this point, only too happy to oblige – being an active part of a successful psychic experience is thrilling, after all – and will willingly apply the cold reader's descriptions to her own life in any way she can.

In this technique, the client isn't just "part of the process" – she unwittingly does most of the work for the psychic, feeding her information that can be tucked away for later use, all while convincing herself that there never was a more accurate psychic.

Example 1

Psychic: I'm seeing a suitcase or a piece of luggage. And...November. Or December. One of the colder months, And there is a spirit who is smiling...does this mean anything to you? It's coming through incredibly clear, but the spirit who is sending it won't tell me anymore.

Client: Luggage or a suitcase? In the winter? I don't know. I don't have anything planned...no one in my family...OH!

Psychic: You have hit on something?

Client: Yes! My daughter is going on a band trip to Disney World after Thanksgiving! Oh my God, and Disney World was my deceased mother's favorite vacation of all time. She must be so happy that Sarah is going on this trip!

Psychic: There it is. She has begun to laugh and dance with happiness. This trip will be blessed.

Example 2

Psychic: I'm receiving images of a musical instrument. Something related to music...musical notes...what is the significance of a trumpet or trombone?

Client: Trumpet or trombone...I don't know...oh wait! One of my great uncles played tuba in a symphony orchestra until the day he died. Could that be it?

Psychic: A tuba, yes, that's the instrument...hold on...your Uncle Fred was wondering if you remembered the stories about him? He doesn't want you to forget them.

Client: I won't forget them! I never got to meet my Uncle Fred, but he will always live on in our family because of the stories.

6.   Back to the Past

As the psychic and the client inch their way deeper into the cold reading, the tricks that the psychic uses are ever more honed and subtle. When the reading begins to take on its bulk, so to speak, there are more chances for the psychic to ruin the trust she's established with her client.

In fact, in a recent study, two clients of a well-known psychic were invited to watch the videotape of their sessions. It was found, after watching the entire sessions, the psychic had, on average, been correct in one of fourteen of his statements.

The culprit? Selective thinking. The sitters, by using the common psychological phenomenon of thinking selectively, were able to dismiss all the obvious "misses" and wrong guesses. They remembered only the "hits."

The psychic thus knows that her entire reading rests upon making legitimate hits and legitimizing misses.

Back to the past is one of her go-to tools for rectifying a miss. When a psychic is wrong, which if you are to believe the statistics is most of the time, she can reframe any statement and make it "true" by changing the context of her reading by blaming the miss on the past.

It's simple. She might say, "You had an argument with your best friend lately."

The client says, "No that didn't happen."

The psychic says very matter of factly, as if she's just read a teleprompter or the producer-guide out there has spoken into her earphone, "That's strange because I definitely feel a conflict. That must have happened a longer time ago then."

After that, the miss is left behind. The psychic knows the benefits of damage control. She wants the client to forget she ever said anything. Moving on.

Example 1

Psychic: You had a break-up recently.

Client: Um…no, I've been single for a while now.

Psychic: Ah, of course. I was picking up the energy from when it happened all those months ago. You're a survivor, whether it's break-ups, family tragedies…you always find the strength to pick yourself up and move on.

Client: I do, it's true.

Example 2

Psychic: Someone close to you or near to your family has died in the last year.

Client: (thinking) No…it's been a good year. No deaths.

Psychic: That's odd. I definitely received a signal that suggested someone passing. Perhaps it was a relative or friend who passed long ago, but wants to be remembered.

7.   Question Veiled as a Statement

After a miss, the psychic needs to go back to her bag of tricks. Knowing that direct questions, like the one above, often backfire, she must immediately re-establish her credibility.

Asking a question as if it were a statement is one of the best tools of the trade to get a psychic back on track and running again. Because she knows that the client is willing to selectively dismiss the misses, she still has the confidence of a lion but she has to quickly get herself back on course before she loses the client's trust.

Some of the obvious questions that act as statements are:

"Does this sound right?"

"Please?"

"Can you see why this might be the impression I'm getting?"

"This is along the right lines for you, yes?"

The beauty of this technique is that the psychic can avoid direct questions and also make her questions sound like affirmations.

As an example, let's say the cold reader, through some of her fishing strategies has heard a hint that a wife doesn't feel secure in her relationship.

Instead of asking her why – because how could that possibly be construed as psychic? – she will make a leading statement. These are directly related to the leading questions that are always overruled in court.

In this case, the psychic might say, "I am feeling something interesting here. I wonder why I have this feeling that your husband hasn't been faithful to you."

"That's because he hasn't. I caught him in a lie."

"Yes! That explains why the message was coming through."

In the end, everyone is happy. The psychic has made a hit, albeit through tweaking perceptions. And the client relaxes. This psychic knows her stuff.

Example 1

Psychic: There is a really interesting energy in the room right now. It's very female-centric, but it's tense, like an argument or a disagreement with another woman in your life…would you understand?

Client: Wow, yes, actually. I'm having a fight with my mother about staying with my current boyfriend.

Psychic: It makes sense now. She doesn't think he's good enough for you…this is the cause of the tension, yes?

Client: He's unemployed right now, so I'm supporting both of us, but it's only temporary. He just needs my support to get back on his feet, but she disapproves and thinks he's holding me back.

Example 2

Psychic: I'm feeling there's a loss in your life. It could be a death or simply someone or something was there and now is no longer a part of your life. Is this a feeling that you are having at the moment?

Client: It IS. I was just cleaning the other day and I set down my grandmother's engagement ring. I finished scrubbing...and it wasn't where I left it. I've been feeling terribly about it, I can't stop thinking about it.

Psychic: You had a special connection with your grandmother, isn't that so?

Client: It is. I wear that ring every day to remind me of her.

8.   Wanted To But Didn't Do It

There are other ways the cold reader can undo a miss or strike it right the first time. How the psychic carries on the reading is always dependent on the things the client says, how they are said, and how the psychic can then out-maneuver the client by molding result to fit the scheme.

Sometimes the psychic will say something like: "I'm getting that you've taken a vacation lately."

Then the client says, "Well, no. I couldn't because I had to work."

The psychic doesn't let a second go by. She comes back quickly with the classic "Yes, but I sense you *wanted* to take one."

Out of context, this might seem ineffective, even feeble. But one has to remember. The psychic's studio is a rarified environment. It's a created space, outfitted in a way that accommodates people who are in want of help; people who are vulnerable and willing to believe. In any other setting, this comeback probably wouldn't work. But people who contact a psychic *need* to find an answer. They are almost always willing to hear what they need to hear.

Example 1

Psychic: I am picking up an energy that says you have switched jobs recently or received a promotion.

Client: Actually, no, I have been at this job for a few years.

Psychic: But in fact you have been thinking about how your work deserves greater recognition than it currently receives?

Client: Well...yes, actually. Junior employees are being hired and are making slightly more than I am, and I've been there almost two years now. It's really frustrating.

Example 2

Psychic: There's a spirit in the room which is suggesting that you went to the doctor recently.

Client: No...I haven't gone for myself in a while.

Psychic: Hmm, the doctor's office is coming through very clearly. You need to make one for something, don't you? For you or for someone else in your family?

Client: …yes. Actually, I keep picking up the phone and putting it back down. I almost prefer not knowing.

9.   The Questions Begin

After employing various techniques like shotgunning, the Barnum Effect and making the client part of the process, the psychic should be on fairly stable footing at this point.

The fact is that by this time she has likely persuaded the subject to trust her. She has already made a few "hits" even if she hasn't *really*. At the very least, she's turned her misses into information selected and construed by the client to be true.

Now she can ask some questions to extract information. She can be a little more specific, but with some conditions. For instance, she will ask a question that follows a statement. And, by now it's fairly clear that the statement will be vague since most psychics know they cannot afford the luxury of concreteness.

She might saying something like: "Your sister seems to love you but she doesn't seem to know how to express it. Does this make sense to you?"

Perhaps the client will respond in the negative. "No, I think she genuinely doesn't love me."

The psychic will keep going until she gets the hit. "Yes, I'm feeling a strong sense of anger and jealousy that has manifested as hatred. Would you understand?"

Now the client may nod her head. "Yes. She gets so angry to the point that she throws things."

"Of course!" the psychic will say. "She exhibits anger that can be construed as hatred, when in reality she feels lonely and abandoned. I sensed that from the beginning."

As usual, the psychic scores points even if she hasn't quite nailed it. And most importantly, she now has a road to travel. The conflict here is between the client and the sister. A few more techniques in play will reveal the exact nature of the issue, or at least get closer to allowing the psychic to make her prediction at will.

Example 1

Psychic: I'm getting a strong sense that it troubles you when there are topics where your husband cannot seem to express himself or he shuts down.

Client: Actually, he's quite good on that front. He's perhaps the only man alive who is comfortable expressing his emotions.

Psychic: Yes, he's vocal and surprisingly easy to talk to. It's what you drew you to him in the first place, isn't it?

Client: Absolutely. It's such a rare quality in a man these days. Although…now that I think about it, he does have a hard time discussing work problems with me.

Psychic: Of course, that's the topic where he shuts down. And you just want to be there for him, even if you can't solve the issues.

Example 2

Psychic: I'm sensing that money is the cause of friction for you. Perhaps internally or with your husband.

Client: No...I mean, we're fairly comfortable, thank goodness.

Psychic: But you sometimes spend money on things that you don't need and it can be frustrating to others close to you.

Client: Well...I mean, now and then I'll buy a bunch of stuff online and my husband will get annoyed.

Psychic: He lets a lot of things go, but that in particular bugs him, doesn't it?

Client: Now that I think about it...money does seem to be the one thing that we argue about regularly.

10.   Back to the Future

The cold reading psychic is the ultimate time traveler. If she can't get the past right with her probing and prodding, and she hasn't quite put a fix on the present there is always the future. The safety net is that she won't be wrong in the moment because no one can see the future. Except her, of course.

Let's say, just for fun, the psychic has made a mistake. She is receiving information from the Dolphin animal spirit, who along with speed, diligence and intelligence is the messenger of love. The client is about to take a relationship one step further.

But, oops, the client isn't in a relationship currently. So the psychic travels to the past and suggests, as a question, that the past relationship will be revisited. The client shakes her head in the negative. That was a divorce that she welcomed. The psychic has to take her love bus to the future in a way that will seem like a hit. "Oh, I see that now, yes, I sense that a new love will evolve in the near future."

She may point out her mistake by suggesting how different the new love will be from her ex-husband, thus explaining why the ex-husband came to her at all.

Example 1

Psychic: I'm sensing an illness or a sickness for someone in your family, on the male side...a father or grandfather. Someone older and male.

Client: My family are all, thankfully, quite well at the moment.

Psychic: Hmm, this feeling is persisting for me, though. Was there a serious illness for an older male relative in the past? A hospital stay?

Client: No, not for years and years. The men in my family are quite hearty and live to advanced ages.

Psychic: Wait...wait, yes, I see it more clearly now. There is an illness coming for one of your family, one of the older men. I do see a hospital, but also the love and support of all your relatives getting that member through.

Example 2

Psychic: There is an energy that suggests animals...is there an animal, a pet of some sort, that you are close to at the moment?

Client: No, I don't have any pets right now. It's been years.

Psychic: It must be a family pet from when you were a child. I hear barking and see a wet, black nose, like a dog.

Client: We didn't have any dogs when I was a kid. We only had cats. I always wanted a pup, though.

Psychic: Your desire for a dog, even when you were a child, is strong today. I definitely see a dog in your future, and – it's accompanied by a man! You're going to date someone with a dog and finally get to experience the joys of dog ownership.

11.   Generic Mumbo Jumbo

Only a psychic could get away with an office that contains, among other disparate objects, a Buddha statue, a crystal ball and a smudge pot. This would be talisman overload in any other place, where those not seeking the help of a psychic might be offended at such an odd array of opposing spiritual props. But the psychic, whose bendy spirituality is accepted, can and does get away with inanity. She has to cover all bases by appealing to the largest swath of believers as possible.

It's a truism: when a sitter seeks a psychic because he is worried about finances or a crumbling marriage, he isn't likely to take notice of the disparate and varied ornaments of the trade. The peculiarity of a Buddha statue next to a crystal ball might be lost on him, as he's drowning in the misery of Bankruptcy Court.

So the unruly mumbo-jumboism of the psychic has a real place both tangibly and intangibly in a cold reading.

The psychic who needs to always cover herself in terms of misses, will often say something that contains two generic but opposing statements.

Take the relationship issue. The client says he's been trying to start a relationship with someone. He really likes her. But she's moody and unpredictable, sometimes even dismissive.

The psychic might say, "I sense she has some issues but I also see she has a good heart. If you want this to work in the future, you need to take that into consideration.

Example 1

Psychic: You're experiencing hard times in your marriage right now, aren't you? Things seemed so great, but now it's like a hill crumbling beneath you.

Client: My wife just hasn't been herself lately. Even the kids are picking up on it.

Psychic: Your wife has always been a strong woman on the surface, but even she is fragile deep down. You have to show her that you can appreciate both aspects of her being.

Client: I'm really trying, but it's so difficult to put up with her mood swings.

Psychic: You can work with her extremes up to a point, but you also have to keep in mind your emotional needs.

Example 2

Psychic: There is something stopping you from doing the right thing, isn't there?

Client: How did you know? I'm stuck. I caught an acquaintance's boyfriend cheating on her. I don't know her that well, but my friend is close enough to her that she and I do say hi when we see each other at restaurants or stores.

Psychic: Deep down she knows something is going on, but you telling her or confiding in your mutual friend – who might then tell her – makes it real. You must consider her broken heart as you decide how to proceed.

12.   Making Your Psychic Right – Always

As we've seen, the psychic will enact all manner of ways to avoid the client thinking he's wrong. One of the best tactics is the technique that pushes a client to pony up an endorsement.

Because the sitter wants answers, she is likely also going to want to please the person who gives them to her. This works in the psychic's favor all the time when he makes a mistake.

One of the best ways is to maneuver the client into actually bending over backwards to make the psychic right. For instance, take the following example:

The cold reader will say something like: "I sense that it's not the first time she's done something like that."

The client will say, "No, actually she's never done that."

The psychic, who is also a talented stage actor will act puzzled, twisting his expression into one of confusion. This baffled appearance might put the client on the hot seat. The cold reader will let it sit for a second (and only a second because given too much time, clients will start to think) and say, "This is so strange because it really is coming across very strongly here. Maybe this happened in the past?"

The client will look relieved. "As a matter of fact, my friend told me she *wanted* to do it before."

The cold reader's bewildered expression will fade. All is well. He will say, "Ah, yes. That's what I was sensing. It's perfectly clear now."

And then he rapidly moves on.

Example 1

Psychic: I can tell that you have caught your husband looking at other women before.

Client: Well...no, he's always been really attentive to me wherever we are. But this other night it was just...I caught him staring and then he noticed me watching...

Psychic: That is very odd, because...I am picking up this feeling on the back of my neck that there were warning signs before this. Warning signs you perhaps didn't want to see? Because it was too painful to accept?

Client: (pausing, really thinking) I...oh my gosh. Sometimes when we're at a restaurant and he's talking, he'll trail off like he lost his train of thought. He must be looking at someone with his peripherals!

Psychic: Yes, that must be what I was picking up.

Example 2

Psychic: I can see that you are concerned about your kids. They are growing wild, aren't they?

Client: Yes, it's getting to be too much to handle. I caught my daughter sneaking out last night.

Psychic: It's not the first time she's done it, is it?

Client: Well…I really think it is. The door was so loud when she tried to escape, it woke me up.

Psychic: Hmm, this rebellion is coming across very clearly as a repetitive act. Or as a mutiny long in the making.

Client: Oh! That *does* make sense, then. I've made her miss a few parties, and I could tell she *wanted* to sneak out, but didn't have the guts yet.

13.   Rationalization

How do you placate and divert someone's attention that doesn't agree with you? The psychic knows. He rationalizes and flatters all in one quick sentence. This technique is a first-rate ticket out of blunderville. It's so simple as to go almost unnoticed.

Let's say, for example, the cold reader makes a comment to the client about some recent behavior on his part, one that the client unequivocally does not accept. The psychic will realize there is no way to turn it into gravy for her so instead she might tell the client that he had the potential for that behavior or trait but managed to overcome it. Then she will applaud her client for his growth and restraint

Example 1:

Cold Reader: You have been a bit angry with your children lately.

Client: No, that's not true at all.

Cold Reader: What I mean was that this was something you've overcome which is why it is no longer an issue for you. I was sensing your past. This is wonderful news about you that you should be proud of.

Example 2:

Psychic: In recent times you have been at odds with someone in the workplace. Almost like rivals.

Client: No, everything is really good there. There's a good rapport with all coworkers.

Psychic: Of course, but my sense is that it hasn't always been like that. There have been times when things got rather ugly. But you have the maturity and the grace to move past pettiness and focus on what is important – your work. It's really quite exceptional, and your boss has noticed.

14.   Black and White at the Same Time

This is a favorite of the psychic. It's often something he will blurt out while using the Barnum effect. But it also includes an extra step. When the psychic uses a contradictory statement that includes two possibilities for agreement by the client, then she's put herself into a fabulous position. It's got to be either one or the other, as in a statement like this: You are extroverted and outgoing but sometimes shy and vulnerable.

Often the client will choose one to examine. "Yes," she might say, "I am outgoing most of the time."

The cold reader will latch onto this like it's a rope thrown overboard to rescue her. It works quite well. If the client says she's outgoing, the psychic can give her an optimistic reading. "Yes, I sense this about you. It's very strong and it will take your far in your love relationships and career."

The sky's the limit. The sitter might pick up on the career projection, perhaps, thus giving away a good load of information for the client to work with.

If the customer admits to feeling introverted or shy, never fear. The psychic has solutions.

Either way, the cold read is on at this point and the psychic has made a good connection with the client...and her messengers from the spirit world.

Example 1

Psychic: You work very hard every day, but you are the type of person who knows what he likes to relax and let go.

Client: It's true, I don't need anything except a glass of wine and a good book to unwind.

Psychic: This helps you to be the kind of person who is at peace with himself. You have your insecurities as everyone does, but you also know who you truly are.

Client: Absolutely. I have always had a good idea of who I am since a young age, even when other people had to "find themselves."

Example 2

Psychic: You have made your house a safe haven, yet occasionally you feel a sense of being misplaced.

Client: Sometimes I do feel as though I have come from another time or place!

Psychic: You're an old soul, it's obvious from your aura. Yet you can still experience things with a freshness and a sense of wonder.

Client: I actually just visited Niagara Falls and I was blown away by the beauty and the power of it nature. It took my breath away.

15. Yes and…

There is a fruitful method to twisting the generic statement from the client to the person the client is talking about. If the cold reader learns that the customer wants to discuss a back stabbing co-worker, then the cold reader has a plethora of opportunities to take the reading into a larger arena.

Let's say the client, when speaking about her co-worker says, "She is not just a gossip but her work performance is terrible."

The cold reader has a plethora of opportunities to invite trust, to flatter and above all else, to validate the client.

The most obvious response is the general statement applied to the subject of the client's distress. The connective tissue is the word "and"

"Yes *and* I'm getting information that's pointing to your co-worker's personal life. She is having private problems and also, I'm sensing she has very low self-esteem. Combined, these things are driving her to act out at *work* and they're affecting her performance."

The psychic might then dispense some advice, knowing that chief among the many reasons for the client's visit is the need to know what steps to take.

Example 1

Psychic: You're here because you are upset about someone's behavior…a female, about your age. Perhaps someone who is vying for your boyfriend's attention?

Client: Yes, that's right. His best friend, who is suddenly getting so territorial after five years. She's calling him and texting him constantly and doesn't invite me out to bar nights with the rest of the group.

Psychic: Ah yes, I sense that she is trying to freeze you out. And she's hoping that if she can isolate your boyfriend from you, he will see how supposedly wonderful she is.

Client: But why?! I have never done anything to her. I have always been nice to her!

Psychic: Yes, but even your kindness is a threat to this woman, because it is in such stark contrast to her own personality. And she suffers from low self-esteem, especially when she is around someone as naturally vibrant and interesting as you.

Example 2

Psychic: (mid-reading) Your sister has been picking fights since your mother decided to take you alone to Ireland with her.

Client: Yes, she's been a total brat. I'm sorry she has college classes and I have vacation days saved up – I'm not going to miss this trip just because she's jealous!

Psychic: Nor should you. This will be a transformational voyage for you, and she feels as though your mother is favoring you. It's been like that all your life, hasn't it?

Client: Pretty much. I don't know what to do with her right now.

Psychic: You are already handling her with grace and tact, and it spurs her jealousy even more because she cannot bait you into petty conflict. Keep on your path and encourage her to keep on hers.

16.   Speaking of Advice

The client wants it, the psychic will give it. And he knows just how to do it. Sticking with the common theme of staying as generic as possible, any and all specific advice has the potential to detonate an otherwise adequate cold read. Of course, since the psychic does very often know the specifics, advice must take the most universal form.

Going back to what we know are the most common reasons people visit a psychic, the cold reader knows that almost one general piece of advice slightly tailored to each reason will work.

Love problem? Here's the advice: "You must be patient and kind. Use your best qualities and be helpful."

Career problem? Here's the advice" "You must be patient and kind. Use your best qualities and be helpful."

And so on.

Example 1

Psychic: With your mother so sick, you are here to learn what you should do moving forward.

Client: That's right. Everything is in disarray, my siblings are all fighting, and I feel like the sole voice of reason while she lies dying on that hospital bed.

Psychic: The spirits around us tell me that you are your family's only hope in these hard times. You must stay strong, even in the face of the worst troubles. Summon all your patience and hold to it. If you devolve into petty squabbles with your siblings, your family will suffer the worse for it.

Client: I'll do whatever I have to. I can see now that I am the family's backbone right now.

Example 2

Psychic: You feel as though your relationship is stalled because your boyfriend has not yet proposed.

Client: It just seems like, if he wants to be with me, he'll put a ring on my finger. I've been waiting for five years.

Psychic: You must be aware of how strong your energy is and how frightening it can be to have someone love you as deeply as you love him. You must be patient and know that it will happen if it is meant to happen. Show him your love every day as a gentle reminder how lucky he is.

17.   Be Mysterious

It's always good times in the psychic chair. The clairvoyant in every psychic likes to throw out a mysterious prediction, which tends to intrigue folks looking to lift their lives out of the doldrums.

So a cold reader, usually at the end when everyone is happy with the reading, might say, "Oh wait. I'm sensing something interesting. Yes. I'm getting information that you'll be exploring the pyramids in Egypt and that the experience will change your life."

The plot thickens for this lucky client.

Example 1

Psychic: Before you go...ahh...one moment...there is something coming through finally that has been simmering underneath for the duration...

Client: Oh! What is it?

Psychic: I'm getting...a new stranger in your life. Someone you may have heard of before but never met. You will meet this person within the next year and they will change the course of your life forever in ways you can't imagine.

Client: So exciting!

Example 2

Psychic: The wildest notion is striking me now, right before you go.

Client: What is it?!

Psychic: Running shoes. Athletic shoes. Not necessarily for sports, but...shoes that are hardy and can handle a journey. They are sturdy and comfortable. There is something far-flung in your future and you have to be ready for it or the opportunity will be lost.

Client: I cannot wait to find out what is in store for me!

18.   Always say yes to the negative

This is a classic technique that will *always* work. When a client says something negative about someone in their lives, the psychic will always agree.

The client says: "I think my stepfather is envious of my success, that's why he doesn't like me."

The psychic will reply to this one immediately: "Yes! That's a very astute observation. He regrets that he failed to accomplish so much in his life. And when he sees your success those regrets bubble to the surface."

Everyone loves validation.

Example 1

Psychic: There is some rivalry coming up on my radar, so to speak. A competition with another female member of your family.

Client: Of course, my sister. She is always trying to outdo me in everything, but it just makes her look foolish.

Psychic: Yes, you are absolutely right. That is how everyone – even some of the other members of your family – view her pettiness. It is hard for her to have a sister so naturally accomplished and well-liked, so she overcompensates to her own detriment.

Client: I thought it was just me seeing this!

Example 2

Psychic: A friend is in a relationship and you have doubts about things she cannot seem to see.

Client: Yes! I have told her again and again, as nicely as I can, that he is using her. She won't listen to me.

Psychic: She had better listen to you – you are guided by the spirits now, and you are absolutely correct in your assessment. He is taking advantage of her and hopes that those around her won't notice. Beware him trying to cut you and her other friends out, so his influence can grow.

Client: I thought he was doing that! He makes her check-in with him every time we hang out, to the point where she is starting to say that she would rather just stay in.

19.   The Mysterious Number

Cold readers are not just allowed to be mysterious. Mysteriousness is expected of them. Whereas a doctor might find himself in a medical malpractice suit for handing out inscrutable information, a psychic might get dinged on her Yelp reviews if she doesn't.

So one of the things she likes to do is throw out a number, any number, and see what the cat drags in. The trick for the cold reader is to acknowledge that he doesn't know what the number means but that surely it will be revealed at work. Or in the client's love life. Or on the customer's trip to Vegas.

Example 1

Psychic: There is a strong message coming through...and it concerns the number 42.

Client: 42? I...I have no idea. What does it mean?

Psychic: It is difficult to say, because the spirit sending this message is not telling me any more than that you should be aware of the number 42. And...wait...it has something to do with travel. Perhaps the age at which you will take a dream trip? Or it might be the seat number where you sit on the plane.

Client: Number 42. I won't forget it.

Example 2

Psychic: The number 18 is deeply significant for some reason. What is this reason? It is being repeated over and over again.

Client: I can't think why. Hmm…

Psychic: It's the number 18 and is full of love. It's a very loving number.

Client: Oh! My son is going to turn 18 this year! We've been talking about where to hold his birthday party, because we want to make it very special.

Psychic: There it is. That's why the number has been resonating through the room since you arrived.

20.   The Name Game

The well-informed cold reader has committed to memory the five most common names of every generation, including among Latino, Asian and other immigrant communities. All it takes is a little studying and the ability to guess someone's age.

So somewhere along the cold read, especially if it's stalled, the psychic might throw out a common name and fish around for some clues and some viable information. If the client doesn't respond, the cold reader will correct herself, claiming that this name will appear in the future. But usually the customer can come up with something that will give the psychic a chance to make some inroads into the problem. The hope, of course, is to get to a solution, which usually is addressed in some of the other various techniques examined above.

As with any time the psychic is wrong or doesn't make a hit, he can always do the old bait and switch. In this case, if wrong, the cold reader will attribute the name to someone else, perhaps the client's girlfriend or, to be very safe, a distant relative.

Example 1

Psychic: The energy around you is giving me a name…Jessica? Jessie? Jennica? Perhaps even Jenny or Jennifer? Definitely a J name, someone close to you, a good friend or relative.

Client: Oh my gosh, could it be my friend Jessica? She's getting married next week and I'm a bridesmaid in her wedding!

Psychic: Jessica, that's it. I thought so. You were instrumental in bringing about this wedding, weren't you? You introduced them or…when they were introduced and dating, you often dispensed advice to Jessica that she took very much to heart.

Client: We used to talk about her fiance all the time when they would go through rough patches. I told her to just see it through, because they were meant for each other.

Psychic: You did very right by your friend Jessica, the spirits are telling me. You should be proud of yourself for helping your friend.

Example 2

Psychic: There is a name that is going unsaid, but I am going to bring it up. Tom. Thomas. Perhaps even Timothy or Tim. A hard T-sound and a male who is close to you, or who was close to you and is no longer.

Client: Oh dear. My father. Thomas. He passed just last year, and I'm still devastated by it.

Psychic: Of course, it's becoming so much clearer. You feel as though there were things left unsaid or undone.

Client: We always said we'd take a trip to Rome together, but the cancer was so aggressive…

Psychic: My dear, he wants you to take that trip and imagine you are seeing it through his eyes.

21.   The Meaning is on the Client

When in doubt, the cold reader will shift meaning onto the client. This means that after a general statement, it's up to the client to state whatever meaning the statement has for him. This gentle prodding trick allows the psychic to stay off the hook, but also possibly acquire more information.

Let's say the cold reader already knows that the client's grandmother has passed. She might follow up with a statement like this: "Your grandmother passed due to problems in her chest or her stomach."

Knowing that the main causes of death in women is heart disease, usually followed by cancer, the cold reader has likely landed on something. But perhaps, as might be discovered, neither of these outcomes were in evidence, then maybe the reference to chest issues could mean a broken heart, or being tired. Anything will work and the psychic is always there to lend a helping hand by gently leading the customer to give up more information.

Example 1

Psychic: We know your brother moved to another country...your brother...I'm picking up something about him. Does he have stomach problems of some sort?

Client: No, not that I know of...he's usually in good health.

Psychic: I'm definitely picking up something having to do with his stomach...sick to his stomach...deep down in his stomach...is there some reason this could be?

Client: Well, I...the thing is, I thought it seemed as though he didn't want to go, but had to for work. I know he's homesick.

Psychic: Ah, there it is. He's sick to his stomach about missing his family back home, but doesn't want to say anything for fear of seeming weak. So he's pushing it deep down. Be there for him as much as you can.

Example 2

Psychic: Has someone in your immediate circle suffered a broken bone? An arm, a leg...maybe even a rib.

Client: I can't think of anyone.

Psychic: (knowingly) Something has been broken in a family member or friend, and they are suffering with stoicism. Perhaps that is why you aren't even aware. Can you think of anyone?

Client: Well...I...actually, a friend of mine just got left by her husband. And her exact words were, "He has broken my heart and my spirit." That must be it.

Psychic: That IS it. It's much more obvious now. She is in so much pain it feels as though she is literally broken. You have to help support her emotionally or she will never mend.

22.   Symbolism is the Psychic's Best Friend

A symbol that arises out of the psychic sky is a fantastic way for a psychic to lead the client on to feel dialed into that world that up till now, only the clairvoyant knows. This is the ultimate way to make the sitter feel like she is part of the process.

The cold reader might use one of the most common symbols known to psychics: The Dragonfly.

In using symbols the cold reader has to educate the customer while he is bringing forth this majestic symbol from the spirit world.

Psychic: "I am seeing a dragonfly. The dragonfly is one of the most common gateways to the spirit world. And it's a creature that is flexible, adaptable. It suggests transformation, peace and tranquility. In my vision, the dragonfly is looking at you, it wants you to follow it into this safe, lovely world."

What more would a client want to believe than that this little critter from the psychic heavens want her to be peaceful?

There are other great symbols for the cold reader to invoke:

A path

A fork in the road

Mountains

The pause button on your remote control device

A bridge

The list is endless. But these common symbols are sure conversation starter; as with any symbol, they can mean almost anything. This is a highly productive way for the psychic to learn more about the client.

Example 1

Psychic: A strong symbol is coming through, it has come through since you sat before me. You may laugh, but I am seeing a dog. A sweet little dog, who sits and waits patiently for his master. He is sad but hopeful and brimming with love, knowing that is only a matter of time, though time seems to be moving so slowly.

Client: Wow, I…I have been waiting for my boyfriend to propose. We have been talking about getting engaged…

Psychic: Of course, that is what I am seeing. The dog represents your loyalty, your faithfulness. It knows that waiting patiently is always rewarded.

Example 2

Psychic: I am seeing a rose. It's so fragrant, I can almost smell it, I can nearly feel the silky softness of its petals. It is an exquisite creation that brightens the lives of everyone who sees it. It is a single rose is almost heartbreakingly perfect.

Client: I…I just found out that I'm pregnant with a girl! A few days ago, actually. She is my little rose!

Psychic: She will be outstandingly beautiful in your eyes, and not a day goes by when you will not appreciate the light she brings into your life, while also recognizing the fragility of our human bodies.

23.   State Questions Negatively

Normally emphasizing the negative only reminds people of what they do or do not have, but in cold reading, it can be cleverly used to validate the sitter or invite them to share more information. You won't simply be pointing out the bad in your client's life, though; you will frame the negative as part of a question, like, "There haven't been many accolades coming your way at work lately, have there?" Your sitter feels as though you understand exactly how they are feeling, and the question format opens the door for them to share more information that can be used immediately or saved for later.

Example 1

Psychic: You haven't been feeling very appreciated at home, have you?

Client: (near tears) It's been…incredibly difficult since we had the new baby. I might as well be my family's servant.

Psychic: I sensed your fatigue the moment you walked in here. They don't seem to realize how lucky they are to have you watching out for everyone, do they?

Client: No. I really think they don't.

Example 2

Psychic: There haven't been many dates on the horizon lately, have there?

Client: No...I have been laying low lately. I don't know, kind of in a funk, I doubt I will ever meet the right girl.

Psychic: I thought I felt a depressive, rather glum aura emanating from you. But you cannot really think that someone as attractive, warm and humorous as you will be single forever, do you?

Client: I...I guess not. But it's just such a rat race. They want guys with big houses and flashy cars.

Psychic: Not all women, not by a long shot. Most women want a man who will love them and be loyal to them. You are capable of all that, and more.

Closing the Session

As discussed, people go to psychics when their lives are falling apart, or some aspect of their lives has hit a bottom. It goes without saying that when life is good, folks party, they don't end up on the psychic's couch.

What people want is comfort; the sort of thing that they can't find elsewhere for whatever reason. They want understanding, maybe the tough love approach of an absent father, or the calm, loving stroke of an auntie.

But most of all, people want to know the future. If only we could all divine what's in store for us, then maybe we could change things, move forward, embrace life, have hope.

Psychics trade in hope. And they know that the "whole package" of a cold reading hits its apex with a prediction. No reading is complete without one.

Predictions, like anything else the psychic puts forth in her reading, have to seem specific, though they *must* be general. The skilled psychic will also throw a monkey wrench into the prediction, just to make it appear realistic.

For instance, as we know, a psychic's credibility will be destroyed if she tells her client that everything will be fantastic. In order to appear rational and super dialed into the world of the spirits, she has to make sure she doesn't overdo the prediction.

At the end of the reading, for example, the client might ask what she can expect for the future.

This is theater time for the psychic. He might say something like this: "The big news that I have discovered about you (here he might insert the client's name in) is that a very important event will happen soon. During the reading, I have been gathering sensory information, and the good news is that you will be under the influence of a rare and intense period of transition. The transition period will take 47 days, and at the end, you will…"

Here the psychic will insert the relevant information: start interviewing for jobs, or begin meeting new men, or your health will begin to improve.

Notice that even in the final moment of the prediction, there isn't a positive, easily confirmed prediction. The psychic starts with a nebulous number of "transition" days, followed by some very vague activities and improvements that are more than likely going to happen.

The other prediction strategy occurs when the clients asks a specific question. For instance the client might say, "Will the employer grant me an interview?"

The psychic will say, "Yes."

Client: "Will this happen in the next week?"

Psychic: "No. What I am sensing is that it will take time, but that there will be an interview within two to three weeks."

The psychic appears to have directly answered the question in a most positive way for the client, and has reaffirmed her trustworthiness by throwing in a no. This "no" brings in unexpected changes, which most people trust because life is capricious that way. The client will be comforted – a job interview is coming – but the psychic hasn't really committed to anything except to a game of realistic-seeming semantics that make the customer feel assured and at ease. The psychic is happy too since he can safely predict that he's just garnered a repeat customer.

Conclusion

While there are no hard statistics out on the number of people who have visited a psychic, evidence abounds that psychics today are alive and well. They are on television, in pop-up street corner bodegas, in homes and buildings. The Internet is a virtual smorgasbord of choices. Get free readings, phone readings, psychic tweets, email clairvoyance. You name it, they've got it.

For some people, visiting a psychic is a normal every day occurrence. For others, desperation has driven them there. But no matter the reason, it is almost impossible to ignore that cold readings are virtually meaningless.

There is so much evidence to support that a psychic is an expert manipulator. Even psychics who believe they are psychic, are still using the very same tactics exposed here. Scientific experiments that copy the psychic's techniques in all their various forms indicate that pretty much anyone who wants to practice the skills and commit a few statistics to memory can give a cold read.

Is it intuition or practiced skill? Certainly people have honed their ability to detect body language and facial expressions. We can train ourselves to hear notes of worry or distress or joy in the voices of those around us. We know the smell of cigarette smoke on someone's sweater, expensive perfume, nice shoes and we know their opposites. These clues are the first impressions that a psychic uses to choose what secondary tools she will use.

And there is certainly evidence that people have and use intuition otherwise known as wisdom. Science has proven this. We know, for instance, when to run from someone because our hearts race when they walk behind us. We make life and death decisions, often to our benefit. We know intuitively that someone is almost always coming around that blind corner. Many scientists have even concluded that intuition is more biologically plausible than logic, simply because it is theory free and does not require high-level logic models.

But there is no empirical data that anyone who isn't schizophrenic or on hallucinogenic drugs can commune with the spirit world. None.

So what is this cold read that we speak of?

More rubbish than reality. The fact that anyone can do it argues against specialness or uniqueness.

And the tools of the trade are all used to stage-manage people so that they will give up information that allows the cold reader to get it right one in ten times of stabbing that statement in the dark. In all cases, it's the customer doing all the work as they attempt to find meaning in the various fishing techniques the cold reader uses. Maybe it's really the client who should get paid!

Times are certainly interesting. Our fast-paced techno-world puts more pressure on people to stay on top than ever before. Relationships conducted by texts and working via the Internet are increasingly replacing human to human interaction. So many questions arise. Wars and economy woes, the onset of new illnesses and social mores have made the post 9-11 world difficult to navigate.

Who doesn't want answers? We are all searching for ways to cope, ways to decide, ways to improve. And people who go to psychics are no different except that instead of being the recipient of the news, they are the ones providing it. Cold read clients don't want to seem unhelpful. They don't want to "block" the psychic's power. So they go along with the statements and visions, ever mindful that they are to be helpful. They are willing to acknowledge and agree with semi-truthful statements and back-handed queries. In short, the supposed power of the psychic really arises out of the interaction with the client. This imbalance should certainly give potential customers pause.

www.ingramcontent.com/pod-product-compliance
Lightning Source LLC
Chambersburg PA
CBHW050558280326
41933CB00011B/1896